Purpose Inspired:
Reflections on Conscious Living
VOLUME 3

By Wayne Visser

Paperback edition published in 2020
by Kaleidoscope Futures, Narborough, UK.

Copyright © 2020 Wayne Visser.

All rights reserved. No part of this publication may be reproduced, stored in a retrieval system, or transmitted, in any form or by any means, electronic, mechanical, photocopying, recording or otherwise, except as permitted by the UK Copyright, Designs and Patents Act 1988, without the prior permission of the publisher.

Cover photography and design by Wayne Visser.

Printing and distribution by Lulu.com.

ISBN 978-1-908875-45-7

Non-fiction Books by Wayne Visser

Beyond Reasonable Greed: Why Sustainable Business is a Much Better Idea!

South Africa: Reasons to Believe

Corporate Citizenship in Africa: Lessons from the Past, Paths to the Future

Business Frontiers: Social Responsibility, Sustainable Development and Economic Justice

The A to Z of Corporate Social Responsibility: A Complete Reference Guide to Concepts, Codes and Organisations

Making A Difference: Purpose-Inspired Leadership for Corporate Sustainability & Responsibility

Landmarks for Sustainability

The Top 50 Sustainability Books

The World Guide to CSR: A Country by Country Analysis of Corporate Sustainability and Responsibility

The Age of Responsibility: CSR 2.0 and the New DNA of Business

- The Quest for Sustainable Business: An Epic Journey in Search of Corporate Responsibility
- Corporate Sustainability & Responsibility: An Introductory Text on CSR Theory & Practice – Past, Present & Future
- CSR 2.0: Transforming Corporate Sustainability and Responsibility
- Disrupting the Future: Great Ideas for Creating a Much Better World
- This is Tomorrow: Artists for a Sustainable Future
- Sustainable Frontiers: Unlocking Change Through Business, Leadership and Innovation
- The CSR International Research Compendium: Volumes 1-3
- The World Guide to Sustainable Enterprise: Volumes 1-4
- The Little Book of Quotations on Social Responsibility
- The Little Book of Quotations on Sustainable Business
- The Little Book of Quotations on Transformational Change

Purpose Inspired: Reflections on Conscious Living: Volumes 1-2

Fiction Books by Wayne Visser

I Am An African: Favourite Africa Poems

Wishing Leaves: Favourite Nature Poems

Seize the Day: Favourite Inspirational Poems

String, Donuts, Bubbles and Me: Favourite Philosophical Poems

African Dream: Inspiring Words & Images from the Luminous Continent

Icarus: Favourite Love Poems

Life in Transit: Favourite Travel & Tribute Poems

The Poetry of Business: A CEO's Quest for Meaning

Follow Me! (I'm Lost): The Tale of an Unexpected Leader

About the Author

Dr Wayne Visser is Professor of Integrated Value and holds the Chair in Sustainable Transformation at Antwerp Management School. He is Director of the think-tank and media company, Kaleidoscope Futures and Fellow at Cambridge University's Institute for Sustainability Leadership. His work as a strategy analyst, sustainability advisor, CSR expert, futurist and professional speaker has taken him to 78 countries. Dr Visser is author of 39 books – including *Sustainable Frontiers: Unlocking Change Through Business, Leadership and Innovation*. Dr Visser has been recognised as a top 100 thought-leader in trustworthy business and received the Global CSR Excellence & Leadership Award. He founded CSR International, after obtaining a PhD in corporate social responsibility. He previously served as Director of Sustainability Services for KPMG and Strategy Analyst for Capgemini in South Africa. Dr Visser lives in Cambridge, UK.

Website: www.waynevisser.com

Email: wayne@waynevisser.com

#Connected.

It's 145 years since Alexander Graham Bell spoke his famous words via telephone: 'Mr Watson, come here, I want you'. Since then, the world has grown more connected than Bell could ever have imagined. In a complex system, connectivity creates innovation; so-called emergent behaviour – capabilities and behaviours impossible for the individual parts. That's why we need to work hard to close the digital divide, like gaps in mobile connections (72 vs 123 per 100 people in least developed vs developed countries) and internet access (1 in 5 vs 4 in 5 in least developed vs developed countries). Let's connect.

#Drawdown.

We can meet the Paris Climate Agreement by the mid-2040s. This is the hopeful conclusion from Project Drawdown's 2020 Review. The original 2017 publication Drawdown, edited by Paul Hawken, set out 100 existing climate solutions, evaluated scientifically and ranked in terms of their potential positive impact. The Review updates the ranking of solutions that reduce sources, support sinks and improve society, finding the top 5 solutions are onshore wind, utility-scale solar, reduced food waste, plant-rich diets and health & education. The financial case is also compelling, with net operational savings exceeding net implementation costs four to five times over.

#Women.

When we celebrate International Women's Day, few realise the link to Russia's February Revolution, when women from the textile factories in Saint Petersburg (then Petrograd) went on strike for 'bread and peace'. Seven days later, Tsar Nicholas II abdicated, and the government granted women the right to vote. Today, the Global Gender Gap report shows we still have a long way to go to ensure equal opportunities for women. We have the inspiring role models, like Greta Thunberg, Mary Barra, Sanna Marin, Rose Marcario and Jacinda Arden. But we must continue to support the bottom-up people's movement for change.

#Competition.

Adam Smith's 'invisible hand' of the market is misunderstood – and underrated. Many forget that besides The Wealth of Nations (1776), Smith also wrote The Theory of Moral Sentiments (1759). He argued that markets need a moral context – provided by government regulation – to operate effectively. We are also ignoring his most fundamental requirement: markets need large numbers of small competitors to operate efficiently. Today, the Fortune 500 companies' revenues of $13.7 trillion exceed the cumulative GDP of 184 countries, while Walmart's revenue is bigger than all but the top 27 national economies. Concentration of wealth and power is never good.

#Lawns.

Our suburban lawns (along with golf courses) are green deserts – biodiversity dead zones. While our catastrophic loss of wildlife and insect populations is largely due to industrial agriculture, our cities have also wiped out ecosystem habitats. Douglas Tallamy, in his new book *Nature's Best Hope* points out that lawns are biodiversity unfriendly by design: chemically treated and lacking diverse flora. They are also water-thirsty and poor carbon sinks. If American homeowners converted half their land to native plantings, it would create an area larger than all national parks in the lower 48 states combined. Time for some suburban rewilding.

#Scenarios.

What will happen with the coronavirus? We can't be sure. It's extremely complex and the situation changes day-by-day. That's perfect territory for scenarios. I was reminded of this by scenario strategist and co-author of my first book, Clem Sunter. He sent me his latest scenarios for the epidemic: Much Ado About Nothing (everyone is overreacting); The Camel's Straw (triggers a global recession); and Spain Again (a repeat of the Spanish flu pandemic of 1918 that killed more than 50 million people). Scenarios, unlike forecasts, allow us to imagine, simulate and prepare for different outcomes, adjusting as the future unfolds.

#Pandemic.

Since the WHO declared Coronavirus a pandemic, many interesting (and some frightening) things are going to happen. International travel will collapse, events will be cancelled, supply chains will be severely disrupted, social gatherings will all but disappear, workplaces will become ghost-towns, food shortages will occur (mostly due to panic buying) – and despite all of this, a lot of people will be sick. This is classic emergence behaviour in self-organising systems, where local information becomes the strongest driver: copy-thy-neighbour is the new organising principle. As this ripples through the system, it creates waves of tipping points. Buckle-up! Storms ahead.

#Calm.

DON'T PANIC! These are the words on the cover of The Hitchhiker's Guide to the Galaxy (in Douglas Adam's sci-fi book of the same name). It's advice we could all heed right now, as Coronavirus COVID-19 wreaks havoc with our lives. Put another way: Keep Calm and Carry On. This meme comes from a 1939 British government poster during the lead-up to World War II. We're fighting another kind of war right now and the coming weeks and months will require level heads, but also open hearts. Let's not panic. But most of all, let's look after one other.

#Here.

When the world 'out there' seems to be swirling out of control, it helps to zone in on your own world 'right here'. Get local. How is your home, your family, your garden, your friends? Notice the simple things: the spring flowers or the autumn leaves, the reliable postman or the chatty shopkeeper, the tail-wagging dog or the curled-up cat. When you focus on what's right in front of you, or immediately around you, you gain perspective. It becomes clearer what needs doing. You take back power. Anxiety goes down. You are grateful for simple pleasures and small blessings.

#Harmony.

When chaos enters our lives, it is good to remember that there is a deep underlying harmony in the universe. Einstein was profoundly inspired by Mozart, whose music he said revealed a 'pre-established harmony'. While the scientific ideas of his contemporaries lacked the 'architecture' and 'inner unity' that Mozart's music embodied, his theory of relativity was an attempt to bring us closer to the 'harmony of the spheres'. Similarly, HRH The Prince of Wales' book *Harmony*, written with Tony Juniper and Ian Skelly, encourages us to apply the principles of balance and proportion to more positively impact the world.

#Experts.

Now more than ever, we need to listen to science, to ask for evidence, to follow the data. But we must also be wary of how science is being used by politicians and corporates. We see vastly different political strategies to tackle Coronavirus – all claiming to be following expert scientific advice. This is nothing new. When Rachel Carson built her scientific case against the harmful use of herbicides and pesticides in agriculture, the agrochemical industry wheeled out their scientific counter-experts. Big Tobacco and Big Oil have done the same. So let's promote science-based, but remain vigilant about vested interests.

#Pivoting.

As the Coronavirus pandemic continues to turn our lives upside-down, there is a new mantra: pivot to live it. This means rapidly changing tactics, heading in a different direction, or adopting new strategies – and it goes as much for individuals and companies as for governments and social movements. Typically, Millennials and GenZ are more adept at such swift adaptation, as we see with the Fridays for the Future climate protests that have pivoted to #DigitalStrike and #ClimateStrikeOnline, urged by their uber-resilient leader Greta Thunberg. In Asia, they're also redirecting their energies to filing lawsuits. How will you be pivoting?

#Isolation.

Humans are social animals. Like ant colonies, we self-organise based on social interaction. This makes the current requirements for self-isolation and social distancing due to the Coronavirus both biologically unnatural and emotionally challenging. Fortunately, we live in a digitally connected world, where we are still able to reach out to colleagues and loved ones – and we must make a conscious effort to do so, now more than ever. But let us also remember those who are not digital natives, who are not social media savvy, who may not even be connected online. We must stay connected with them too.

#Comeback.

The good news is that nature is making a comeback. The bad news is that it's because travel, tourism, industry and consumption has stalled during the Coronavirus pandemic. NASA has released satellite images showing air pollution over China all but disappearing, while fish have been spotted in the clear waters of Venice's canals. Nature will bounce back if we give it half-a-chance, but a global recession is not a sustainable solution to ecological decline. Rather, we must radically redesign production and consumption to support our quality of life, while giving nature the time and space to recover and thrive.

#Management.

Can we cut the strings of management science? The discipline of management has evolved from the creation of corporations (VOC, 1602) to the introduction of scientific management (Frederick Taylor, 1911), the application of bureaucracy (Max Weber, 1921), the discovery of the employee Hawthorne Effect (Elton Mayo, 1920s) and the introduction of Management by Objectives (Peter Drucker, 1954). But these are all rooted in a mechanistic view of business and a rational view of humans. Isn't it time that we embrace a more holistic, creative management approach based on our contemporary understanding of people and organisations as complex living systems?

#Odd.

For years, I used to wear odd socks. It was an act of rebellion against conformity and societal norms. As social creatures, we humans are predisposed to a herd mentality. Most of us like to fit in rather than stand out from the crowd. This is linked to our deep psychological need for acceptance and belonging. But every now and then, it is good to challenge group-think and choose to be different. And also to respect and celebrate the differences of others. Wearing odd socks on World Down Syndrome Day is one way. How are you a bit odd?

#Rays.

It may seem strange to talk about light during a gloomy global crisis. But this is exactly the time to focus on the positive. When dark clouds threaten to overwhelm us, we all need to seek out – and to share – some rays of sunshine. The key is to understand that happiness is an attitude. Victor Frankl, the Austrian psychiatrist and Nazi concentration camp survivor, understood this well. Even when circumstances are bleak, we can still choose how we respond. When other choices are taken away, we can still adopt a constructive attitude. What bright rays can you share today?

#Transformation.

What does a sustainable transformation look like during a crisis? Here are five signposts: 1) Be resilient – do what it takes to survive; pivot, adapt, bounce back. 2) Be inclusive – help the most vulnerable; volunteer, donate, pool resources. 3) Be frugal – find ways to do more with less; reuse, recycle, go circular. 4) Be connected – use technology to increase communication; e-work, check-in, share solutions. 5) Be healthy – put people's wellbeing first; exercise, de-stress, allow recovery. A crisis is a great opportunity to break the mould, to rapidly test new ways of producing, working and consuming. Let's not waste it.

#Seagrass.

Scientists in Wales are pioneering seagrass restoration as a natural climate solution. Seagrass covers just 0.2% of the ocean but provides 10% of its carbon storage. This remarkable plant stores carbon at 35 times the rate of tropical rainforests and creates habitats for 40 times as much marine life as seabeds without grass. But pollution and shipping are destroying seagrass at an alarming rate (the UK has already lost 90%). Now in Dale Bay, the Seagrass Ocean Rescue project is placing miles of rope with little hessian bags and a million seagrass seeds on the seabed. Regeneration is happening.

#Morality.

This is the time for moral duty to triumph over political expedience. In 1807 when the British Parliament abolished slavery throughout its empire, it was a decision based on morality, not economic consequence or national populism. We face a similar watershed moment today. Will our politicians put the health of their citizens ahead of economic risks and political gains? Will our business leaders prioritise employee welfare over profits? Will our scientists and health professionals embrace open collaboration across boundaries? Will we each of us make personal sacrifices for the common good? Morality is always a choice. Choose right.

#Exponential.

COVID-19 is finally teaching us the nature of exponential growth. It's a painful lesson, but a necessary one: how incremental change seems slow at first (698 new daily cases on 25 January) and then accelerates (48,460 new daily cases on 25 March). The ecological impacts of economic growth over the past 50 years have the same devastating viral curves, as the ICGB's Great Acceleration charts illustrate. Viewed from the Earth's perspective, humans are the out-of-control virus. Exponential growth in a finite system is unsustainable. Period. But remember: solutions – for the pandemic and the sustainability crisis – can also spread virally.

#Smokeless.

At a time when smokers are among the most vulnerable to COVID-19, Philip Morris has doubled down in its commitment to a smoke-free future', set out in its 2020 Letter from the Board to Shareholders. They claim cigarette sales can end within 10 to 15 years in many countries. The plan is to scale up 'smoke-free alternatives', like vaping, which they admit are also 'not risk free'. Still, it's a big shift for an industry that kills 8 million people a year and damages the health of 1.1 billion customers. Is this responsible business, or more smoke and mirrors?

#Amabie.

In the face of adversity, creativity and solidarity flourish. Which may explain the revival of Amabie, a Japanese folklore healing spirit (yōkai). The story goes that in 1846, a local government official on Kyūshū island spotted a strange creature in the ocean – part mermaid, bird and human, with scales, long hair, a beak and three legs – which warned him of a forthcoming disease. Ever since, Amabie has been associated with warding off epidemics. Most who share Amabie's image on social media today are not superstitious. Rather, they're joining a collective declaration on the COVID-19 pandemic: Together, We Will Overcome!

#Novelty.

One of the consequences of lockdown, social distancing and self isolation is boredom. According to 'The Unengaged Mind', a paper by psychologist John Eastwood, boredom can lead to overeating, depression, anxiety, drug and alcohol abuse, and more risk of making mistakes. For our own mental health, it is important that we stay stimulated and engaged, rather than distracted and demotivated. One way is to change our routines. Yesterday, my wife and I discovered a different route for our daily walk. You might change your work, take a course, revive a hobby, cook a new dish or plan an exciting project.

#Algae.

What is solar powered, sequesters carbon and can grow up to 12 feet a day? You guessed it: algae. In some forms, algae are a problem. In rivers, lakes and estuaries, fed by the nitrogen and phosphorous fertiliser runoff, algae blooms in excess, leading to suffocating eutrophication. But as a potential carbon sink and sustainable material, algae are almost miraculous. ALGIX, Inc is using it to create Bloom, a bioplastics foam used in sneakers for adidas and TOMS. Notpla makes edible, biodegradable water sachets, LOLIWARE innovated hyper-compostable straws and Evoware turns algae into cups, wraps and bags. Green is good.

#Swapping.

The Debt for Nature Symposium was part of a hackathon organised by CrowdDoing and Sustainavista at the Skoll World Forum. Providing debt relief for poor countries in exchange for their protection of natural capital, which secures carbon sinks that the world desperately needs, is a great example of sustainable swapping. In Indonesia, Garbage Clinical Insurance offers another sustainable swap: poor communities clean up trash in their neighbourhoods in exchange for health insurance. In China and Turkey, reverse vending machines allow you to deposit recyclable bottles and receive public transport credit. Let's do trading-up instead of trading-off.

#Ants.

We can learn a lot from the leaderless self-organising abilities of ant colonies. Stanford University biologist Deborah Gordon has uncovered five principles: 1. A group must reach a critical mass; too few and no order emerges. 2. The underlying rules of engagement are simple; ants only use ten pheromone signals. 3. Individuals must be free to explore; random encounters alert to new food or incoming danger. 4. Behaviour is adjusted based on pattern detection; ants register the frequency of their encounters. 5. Local information creates global wisdom; ants don't need any big-picture overview, reading their neighbours' signals is enough.

#Normal.

When our life or work is disrupted, we wish for things to get back to normal. After all, there is comfort and security in old habits and familiar routines. And yet moments of discontinuity are also opportunities to pause, reflect and re-evaluate. Are there parts of your disrupted life or work that you would prefer to keep? And are there aspects of your old life or work that you would like to change? Things never return to normal after a crisis. So why not choose how to make it different and better. Reimagine your life, your work, your future.

#Biochar.

How do you can you tackle climate change and increase agricultural yields while decreasing erosion, water use and chemical pollution? The answer is: biochar. Using pyrolysis, agricultural waste is heated in the absence of oxygen and turns to carbon. Husk in Cambodia creates biochar from some of the 150 million tons of rice husks worldwide that are either burnt or left to rot. By ploughing nutrient rich biochar into the soils of smallholder farmers, Husk has increased yields by 40-100% in a single year. And for every ton of biochar that they create, Husk sequesters 1.33 tons of carbon.

#Homegrown.

If you have a garden at home, no matter how small, you can be part of biodiversity restoration. I'm reading 'Nature's Best Hope' by Douglas Tallamy and he presents a compelling vision of Homegrown National Parks, comprising all the urban and suburban gardens in a country, which can provide refuge for insects, birds and wildlife that have been crowded out of rural areas by agriculture and industry. There are two simple guidelines: 1. Plant indigenous species, since these are evolutionarily suited to supporting your ecosystem, and 2. Reduce (or get rid of) your lawn, which is a green desert.

#Renewal.

Hope springs eternal. And every year, spring renews hope. It is almost impossible to witness the revival of nature without a feeling of wellbeing and optimism rising up like sap in our veins – the trees budding with tender green leaves, birds singing brightly in the high branches, flowers waking from their frozen sleep, splashing colour across gardens, fields and roadsides, butterflies flitting and bees buzzing around newly opened blooms. As we struggle through a winter of isolation and fear, slowing down, digging in and digging deep, it's good to remember that this too will pass. Spring's renewal will come.

#Bacteria.

There's good bacteria and bad bacteria – and the good bacteria is helping us with sustainable innovation. Plastic-eating bacteria have been discovered near a bottle recycling plant in Japan and a polluted site in Houston, Texas. These microbes digest PET, the most common plastic waste. Now German scientists have found bacteria that eat polyurethane used in sneakers, a harder to recycle plastic. And it's not just waste solutions that bacteria bring. Nature's Fynd, backed by $80 million from Bill Gates and Al Gore, has just started production of alternative protein grown from bacteria that lives in Yellowstone geothermal hot springs.

#Twins.

Prevention is better than cure, and sustainable design is better than retrofitting. That's where digital twins come in. By creating a detailed virtual representation of products, processes, factories and value chains, companies can simulate the performance of different designs and operating conditions. They are an extension of scenario planning, but at the product and process level. Digital twins allow designers and operators to find efficiencies, to radically reduce resource inputs, improve safety, cut emissions and eliminate waste. One of the leaders in the field, Dassault Systèmes, calls digital twins a 'decision-making cockpit', enabled by the Fourth Industrial Revolution.

#Flows.

Now is a good time to reflect on flows – more specifically, why movement is vital. It's no accident that enforced self-isolation and restricted movement makes us anxious, frustrated, bored and stressed. Complex living systems are not designed to be static. Energy, materials and organisms all flow and interact through the system, keeping it alive. Living systems need borders as well (membranes, in biological terms) but these are porous by design, allowing exchange with the surrounding environment. So too must our social systems (from families to countries) and our natural systems (from gardens to biomes) be designed for dynamic flows.

#Frugal.

Necessity is the mother of invention and the COVID-19 crisis is proof: manufacturers like Tesla, Ford and GE retrofitting factories to produce ventilators, universities rapidly going virtual, orchestras performing via videoconference. Now we need a new wave of creativity: innovation at low cost – or frugal innovation – so that what is needed can quickly scale and be accessible to all. MIT has created a ventilator that can be made for $100 as compared with $30,000 for commercial ventilators – and they are open-sourcing the design. Similarly, Maker's Asylum in India has made a low-cost face shield. This is innovation for inclusion.

#Stimulus.

Turning new economic stimulus packages green is the biggest opportunity for creating a sustainability tipping point since the 2008 financial crisis. In the EU, the stimulus plan is €750 billion and the government has already stated it will support sustainable growth and a green transition. No such assurances have been given for America's $2 trillion stimulus. Even a call by Democrats to make the $250 billion airline bailout conditional on carbon emission reductions was ignored. Obama's 2008 stimulus plan included significant investments in job-creating green energy and infrastructure. If spend we must, let the spending create a better future.

#Habitats.

If we care about biodiversity, we should worry less about species and more about habitats. We are all familiar with Save the Species campaigns – and we should care enough to want to save them. But if we save or restore their habitats the species will save themselves. The problem is that we've taken away or poisoned the land, food, shelter and water that are necessary for fauna and flora to survive. Even in our gardens, we can create thriving habitats: water basins, leaf litter, bee hotels, wild patches, log piles and native trees and flowers. Make homes for wildlife.

#Curves.

Nature favours curves over straight lines. It designs using circles, cylinders, cones and spheres, rather than squares, cubes, triangles and pyramids. That's because nature is dynamic, in a continual dance of interaction and adaptation. Nature is fluid; it flows and grows. And humans are part of nature, which is why we find beauty in organic shapes: spirals and fractals in flowers, currents and waves in clouds. I have a log covered in the patterns left by a wood-boring insect, which is exquisite with its curves and curls, its loops and hoops. There's art in nature for those who look.

#Resurrection.

For some, resurrection has a religious meaning. For me, it's a reminder of the cycles of life and the resilience of nature. Every day, the sun rises, and we have another chance to live and breathe and make a positive impact. Every year, nature awakes from its winter slumber and bursts into life with buds and birdsong, blooms and bees. Every generation, society faces risks and has the strength to rise to the challenge. We may fall, we may fail, but remember the words of the poet extraordinaire Maya Angelou: still, like dust, like air, like hope, we'll rise.

#Icebergs.

On 14 April 1912 at 11.40 pm the 'unsinkable' HMS Titanic hit an iceberg and sank. There are 4 lessons for how we respond to crises: 1) Never believe you are unsinkable, or too big or too smart to fail; arrogance makes you blind. 2) Invest in early warning systems and don't ignore alarm bells; believe the science. 3) What you see is only the tip of the iceberg; most of the problem is invisible. 4) Act early when facing a credible risk; changing direction takes time, and the bigger the organisation, country, or economy, the longer change takes.

#Emperors.

There are leaders who blame, belittle and bully and there leaders who encourage, energise and empower. It seems strange that anyone would follow a leader who is relentlessly self-serving, who always take the credit for success and never takes responsibility for failure. Perhaps they mistake cockiness for confidence and bombast for boldness. Perhaps in times of uncertainty and fear, they prefer hollow promises of certainty and empty gestures of strength. But sooner or later, the charade of self-aggrandising leaders is exposed. Sooner or later, it becomes clear that the emperor isn't wearing any clothes. Thus ends the emperor's reign.

#Insects.

Could insects be the key to lowering the ecological footprint of feeding our pets and livestock? Meat production has huge impacts on carbon, water, pollution and biodiversity. So what if we substituted the crops we grow for livestock and the meat we produce for pets (which is 12% of total meat consumption) with insects? Dutch insect farmers Protix estimate that insect-based foods use 2% of the land and 4% of the water per kg of protein. Hargol FoodTech already make livestock feed from grasshoppers, while the British Veterinary Association says insect-based foods are better for pets than prime steak.

#Adaptation.

Humans are nothing if not adaptable. In fact, adaptation is probably our evolutionary edge as a species. We see adaptation in action every day in response to COVID-19. Individuals and families are adapting to lockdown with modified social behaviour. Companies and industries are adapting to shuttered workplaces and disrupted value chains with creativity and solidarity. Many are reinventing their production lines to provide vital healthcare goods. And governments are adapting with Herculean efforts to support health services and launch economic rescue packages. Post-Corona, we will emerge with the powerful new knowledge that extreme adaptation possible.

#Mystery.

The antidote to boredom is mystery. We all need to spice up our lives with a little intrigue, to disrupt our routines with the unexpected and to question whether we are prisoners of our habits. For me, books promise the greatest mystery of all. Undiscovered worlds, colourful characters, twisting plots and fecund knowledge – all hidden between two covers, waiting to be revealed. Trident, a bookstore in Boulder, Colorado, has taken it one step further. During the COVID-19 crisis, they are selling 'mystery bags' online, each with a selection of used books and a bag of tea or coffee beans.

#Cherries.

'Can you launch rockets from here? Boy, I've done it for years'. Those are words from a song by Tori Amos called Snow Cherries from France. The lilting, nostalgic lyrics have always stuck with me, especially the line that goes 'All that summer we travelled the world, never leaving his own back garden'. Now, during lockdown, many are discovering that very phenomenon: mind-travelling. For some, it is the world of virtual tourism, whether it's Look Up London's tours of the city, or National Geographic's museum exhibition about Jane Goodall. For others, it is reigniting imagination through books and films.

#Entangled.

Rather than wicked problems, we should think of our global challenges as 'entangled'. Wicked implies something evil and tempts us to look for villains. Instead, these problems – like poverty, climate change and ecocide – are more like an entangled ball of twine. How 'knotty' the problem is depends on whether it is loosely or tightly entangled and whether there is convergence or divergence between those tugging at the strings. Simply pulling harder on one string will probably only make it worse. The only way to untangle these problems is to work patiently, locally, carefully and collaboratively at loosening and unravelling.

#Makeover.

Value creation is under the spotlight – and it's getting a makeover. At the AMS-ABIS roundtable we looked at some of the attractive models on offer, from stakeholder value (Robert Phillips), blended value (Jed Emerson) and sustainable value (Stuart L. Hart), to shared value (Mark Kramer) and integrated value (Wayne Visser). We also got a sneak preview of next season's emerging methodologies, including Total Impact (PwC), Integrated Profit & Loss (Impact Institute) and Long Term Value (EY). Each concept and method struts with flair on the business value catwalk - and all are agreed that shareholder value looks increasingly out of fashion.

#Muir.

What greater legacy can we leave than nature itself. John Muir (1838-1914) was one of America's most eloquent and successful advocates for the preservation of wilderness areas, such as the Yosemite and Sequoia National Parks. We should treasure not only these wild spaces, but also the wisdom that Muir gleaned from spending so much time in nature. He understood nature's therapeutic power, reflecting that 'going out … was really going in'. And Muir was a systems thinking pioneer, noting that 'when we try to pick out anything by itself, we find it hitched to everything else in the universe.'

#Scope.

When it comes carbon commitments, scope is mission critical. If a company says they're tackling climate change, or have emission reduction targets, we must always ask: do you include not only Scope 1 (from direct activities) and Scope 2 (indirect, from electricity and heat) but also Scope 3 (from the full value chain, typically the largest)? Microsoft has committed to be Scope 1-3 negative by 2030 and to remove all Scope 1 and 2 carbon emitted since the company was founded in 1975. Similarly, Shell has committed to become a Scope 1-3 net zero emissions energy business by 2050.

#Everything.

If you've ever felt overwhelmed by the sustainability agenda, you're not alone. Nor is it surprising. As Sonia Bonus, Sustainability Manager for Danone, said the other day during an online dialogue, sustainability is 'the art of everything'. That's exciting, but also daunting. The danger is that we lose focus or spread ourselves too thin. I sometimes say that I'm one of the few sustainability generalists left. The agenda is so complex and dynamic now that we need sustainability specialists, who go deeper on an issue that they feel passionate about, fully aware that everything is connected to everything else.

#Proximity.

Is social distancing a misnomer? During the COVID-19 crisis, physical distancing is imperative. But the truth is, we need social proximity more than ever. We need to be reaching out to others, through calls, video-chats, texts, email, or a wave and smile from across the street. A break from the hustle and bustle of city life, or the stresses of the office, and spending more time with family has its own benefits. But our nature is to be social. So at a time when many feel isolated, lonely and sacred, let's make an extra effort to forge human connections.

#Synthesis.

To live is to walk the path of creative tension. Every day, we are pulled in different directions, between order and chaos, between habit and improvisation, between living and dying. Our lives are like a garden: too much control (like manicured lawns) and it's neat, but boring and lifeless; too much freedom (like wild spaces) and it's exciting, but unwieldy and unmanageable. And so we dance the cosmic dance of yin and yang, according to Taoist philosophy; we wrestle with thesis and antithesis, according to Immanuel Kant. And from these is born Tao (the way) and synthesis (transcendent reality).

#Art.

A picture paints a thousand words. In times of crisis, art also reminds us that life is beautiful, that solidarity is powerful and that selfless behaviour is to be celebrated. Whether it is boldly defiant street art that spontaneously appears on pavements and walls, or brightly hopeful rainbow decorations that are made by children and hung in public places, we need art to lift our spirits. Art has an impact because human brains and cultures have adapted to using symbols and narratives. We identify with archetypes like the fearless hero or mother-like caregiver. Art makes our inner life visible.

#Stoic.

During trying times, we can learn a lot from the Greek philosophy of Stoicism, which teaches an attitude of extreme acceptance; fortitude in the face of suffering. Stoics do not forsake happiness; rather they learn to be happy no matter what their external circumstances are. The Buddhist practice of non-attachment is rather similar. Admiral James Stockdale, who survived 7 years as prisoner of war in Vietnam, provides sage advice as well. He advocates embracing the Stockdale Paradox: You must confront the most brutal facts of your current reality, yet always keep faith that you will prevail in the end.

#Tipping.

The COVID-19 crisis is pushing us towards several positive tipping points. One is the reclamation of space in cities for pedestrians and cyclists. Many cities in Europe, from Milan to Brussels, are using the pandemic to accelerate plans to get more cars off the roads, while New York is phasing in 100 miles of car-free streets. Delivery robots and drones are another trend that will likely advance much quicker due to the virus. And virtual meetings, conferences and classrooms are being pressure-tested as never before, forcing technology improvements and behaviour changes that nudge us towards more climate-wise choices post-pandemic.

#Spaceship.

There was a time when economic, social and environmental crises were 'over there' – someone else's problem. Now, breakdowns in one part of the world can rapidly spread to every other part. There is no 'away' anymore. This was already foreseen in the 1960s by Kenneth Boulding, Barbara Ward and Buckminster Fuller who wrote about Spaceship Earth – a closed system where a problem for one is a problem for all and where resources are finite and must be continually recycled. Spaceship thinking also means solutions can be shared globally and breakthroughs can ripple through the system. One Earth. Global Solidarity.

#Consequences.

Every breakthrough technology has its dark side. Thomas Midgley invented leaded fuel and CFCs, which brought improvements in fuel efficiency and refrigeration, but ended up causing lead poisoning and the ozone hole. Biofuels offer a source of low carbon energy but compete for land with agriculture. Renewables and batteries promise an end to climate-warming fossil fuels but are linked to conflict minerals. Social media gives us voice but is used to spread fake news and undermine democracy. We shouldn't reject these technologies, but we must be vigilant about unintended consequences – and work hard to address them.

#Budding.

After the winter, after the rains, there is the promise of budding leaves and blossoms. Buds are a sign of renewal, life returning and potential yet to be fulfilled. And so it is with us. We need the periods of dormancy, of rest and rejuvenation, of breathing deep and drinking long before we re-emerge with new vitality, new dreams, new colours. It may be that the more severely our lives have been pruned back, the more vigorously it will bud with new life. Then, we need only turn our faces towards the light, and we will grow and flourish.

#Discombobulated.

Are you feeling discombobulated? It's a strange word. But then these are strange times. The word means confused or disconcerted, which surely captures the prevailing zeitgeist. We are caught between conflicting yet simultaneous realities: of suffering and tragedy happening all around us to millions of people; and also of healing, rejuvenation and reconnection to family and nature. Some are going through the fire of crisis, stress and overwork, while others are in the quiet eye of the storm, a place of eerie stillness, isolation and inactivity. It is the age of paradox, when apparent contradictions are the new normal.

#Carbon.

Early estimates suggest that global carbon emissions will drop in 2020 by between 5.5% (according to Carbon Brief) and 8% (according to the International Energy Agency), compared to 2019. Before we begin celebrating, think about the disruption we have experienced. We would need this level of reduction (7.6%) every year this decade to stay within 1.5C warming. The message is clear: carbon is still deeply embedded in our economy and our modern lifestyles, and reduced consumption is unlikely to secure a climate safe future. We need radical innovation, supported by a carbon tax and strong government policies on clean tech.

#Choice.

Should consumers be given a choice whether to buy sustainable or not? Or should manufacturers and retailers practice what is called 'choice editing', which means only offering sustainable products? The problem is that almost all sustainable products are more expensive, so most consumers choose not to buy them. Take tuna for example, which accounts for 28% of global seafood sales. Almost 25 years since it was founded, Marine Stewardship Council (MSC) certified sustainable tuna still only makes up 22% of the market. Companies already choice edit for quality, so why not for sustainability? Let's make sustainability the new quality.

#Afforestation.

Wales is growing a forest that will span the length and breadth of the country, joining up existing protected woodlands with large scale tree planting projects. It forms part of the country's low carbon delivery plan and is aiming to plant 10,000 acres per year. Forests are a one-stop-shop of ecological, social and economic benefits. They simultaneously tackle climate change, create biodiversity habitats, provide recreational space, protect water sources, purify the air and prevent soil erosion. Between 1990 and 2015, the top planted forest growers were China (79 billion hectares), USA (26 bn ha) and Russia (20 bn ha).

#Freelance.

For more than a decade, we have been celebrating the gigeconomy – the trend towards flexible, temporary or freelance jobs championed by the likes of Taskrabbit, Uber and AirBnB. For some, freelancing has been a positive choice, to supplement their income or have more control over their work tasks and schedules. For others, it has been a desperate survival tactic, after being made redundant or facing other financial hardship. Now, as the global economy stalls once again, we see the vulnerability of gig workers, who have no sick leave or other social security benefits. The freelance economy needs rethinking.

#Shades.

Forget Fifty Shades of Grey and think 256 shades of grey. That's the power that AI is bringing to healthcare in general and tackling the Coronavirus in particular. Artificial intelligence can analyse a greyscale image from a mammogram or ultrasonic lung scan in a fraction of a second and diagnose abnormalities far more accurately than a radiologist. What's more, AI is not necessarily about replacing doctors and nurses. In fact, a recent survey by MIT and GE found nearly half of U.S. healthcare professionals said AI is boosting their ability to spend time with and provide care to patients.

#Enigma.

Bletchley Park, the World War II British Intelligence site, is famous for cracking Germany's Enigma code, led by the genius Alan Turing. What made the cryptic codes so hard to decipher was their complexity – literally 15 billion trillion possible combinations (that's 15 with 18 zeros). What's more, the code was changed every 24 hours. Isn't that a lot like life? Every day we face new possibilities, fresh surprises, novel connections and unexpected events. Our lives may seem routine, but order on the surface hides a complex cipher of continuous, dynamic interactions. Our lives are a puzzling, fascinating Enigma code.

#Steadfast.

Many things in life are a marathon, not a sprint – and that is especially true of making change happen. A year ago, I began writing Purpose Inspired – a daily reflection about living consciously in business and everyday life. Each is a short post on a different topic. Some are full of facts and figures; others are more philosophical and poetic. But they have a common theme, which is how we can change ourselves and the world for a better, brighter future. 100 words is no big achievement, but 100 words every day for 365 days has sown a habit.

#Planting.

In response to COVID-19, Pakistan is enacting the new triple bottom line: responsibility, resilience and regeneration. Day labourers who have become unemployed during the crisis are being given the option to become 'jungle workers', planting saplings as part of the country's 10 Billion Tree Tsunami programme. Although 500 rupees ($3) per day for planting trees is only half of a typical pre-crisis wage, it is nevertheless an act of responsibility to give people a financial lifeline and the dignity of a job. It is also helping the society and the economy to be more resilient, while regenerating the ecosystem.

#Unilever.

The much-hailed Sustainable Living Plan of Unilever set up under former-CEO Paul Polman has run its course, with some remarkable achievements: 1.3 billion people were reached through health and hygiene programs, 51% of management roles are held by women, 100% of their electricity is renewable and there is zero waste to landfill from their factories. Since 2010, greenhouse gas emissions are down 50%, their waste footprint was cut 32% and 2.34 million women were given access to initiatives to improve their safety, skills and opportunities. The Unilever Compass will take its place, with 15 multi-year priorities and nine imperatives.

#Plastic.

Our skies may be clearer, but single-use plastic is back and booming. This is an entangled problem. Plastic is useful and we need PPE to fight COVID-19, but we cannot keep toxifying our environment. The task of the Alliance to End Plastic Waste and the New Plastics Economy could not be more urgent. Solutions already exist: carbon positive bioplastics, compostable single-use plastics, recyclable PET bottles and polyester textiles and chemical recycling of mixed-grade plastics. But for these solutions to scale, they need economic incentives: carbon pricing, waste taxes, circular economy subsidies, bottle deposit schemes, and better collection and recycling systems.

#Aviation.

Most airplane fleets are grounded and the airline sector is on its knees. But post pandemic, our appetite for travel will return and climate change will loom ever larger as an existential threat to the industry and the world. Commercial aviation accounts for 2% of global carbon emissions and has a pathway to carbon neutrality by 2050. The bigger challenge is how to make the shift more rapidly. Sustainable aviation fuel can reduce CO_2 emissions by 70-100% but remains expensive. Electric planes for short-haul flights and carbon offsetting can help. But we need stronger government incentives and increased public pressure.

#Bioprinting.

3D printing is taking another leap forward with bioprinting: literally printing three-dimensional living objects. One of the pioneers, Inventia Life Science, is printing living cells for pharmaceutical research and medical drug discovery. How does it work? Cells taken from a patient are cultivated and multiplied to create bio-inks, which are printed from a cartridge with an ink-jet nozzle as microdroplets onto a tissue culture plate. Hence, 3D cancer cells can be printed with the same form and structure as in the body and then different drugs can be tested on those cells. Soon, tissues and organs may be 3D-printable.

#Soundscapes.

Close your eyes. What do you hear? Listen to the soundscape that surrounds you. Are any of the sounds you hear unique to where you are? Japan's Ministry of the Environment has created an official list of 100 Soundscapes of Japan. They include, for example, the sound of bamboo rustling, creaking, scraping and tapping in the Sagano Bamboo Forest on the outskirts of Kyoto. In Estonia's Võru county forest, giant wooden megaphones have been installed to amplify the natural sounds of the trees, the bird and the wind. Give your overstimulated eyes a break. You have ears to hear.

#Fungi.

Mushrooms are marvellous – especially those you can't eat, or even see. When you dig into the world of mycorrhizae – fine, hair-like filaments of fungus that attach themselves to the roots of plants and trees – you will be amazed. These mushroom fibres reach out hundreds or thousands of times the length of one tree root, sourcing water and essential nutrients for the plant. They also form a vast underground communications network – the Wood Wide Web – that allow trees to alert each other to threats and provide intensive care to ailing trees or vulnerable offspring, like an intravenous drip boosting nutrients.

#Gravity.

What goes up, must come down. That's the basic principle of gravity-driven renewable energy. And unlike solar, wind, tidal and geothermal sources, gravity systems are able to synchronise energy generation with periods of peak demand. This is the same approach used by hydroelectric power plants, but the social and ecological impacts have put the brakes on hydro schemes. Now Edinburgh-based company Gravitricity Ltd is planning to use abandoned mine shafts to raise and lower weights of 500 to 5,000 tonnes, generating 1MW to 20MW of power. The company also expects its energy storage solution will cost less than lithium batteries.

#Beavers.

The reintroduction of beavers is showing that nature is infinitely better at managing itself than humans are. Beaver dams – and the changing river habitats they create – increase flood control, purify agriculturally-polluted water, raise water levels and create highly effective nitrogen and carbon sinks. The biodiversity dividends are also substantial. Research shows that streams where beavers live attract 75 times more water birds and 2 to 5 times more aquatic life than in undammed sections. In Europe, reintroductions in 161 locations in 24 countries have boosted beaver numbers from 1,200 to 1.2 million since 1900. Rewilding is a win-win solution.

#Population.

According to biologist Paul Ehrlich and author of The Population Bomb, Impact (I) = Population (P) x Affluence (A) x Technology (T). Of these factors, affluence and technology are by far the biggest. A small minority of the world's population in the rich world is responsible for the biggest ecological impacts, due to our lifestyle, diets, overconsumption and agricultural and industrial practices. Population will stabilise as people come out of poverty, get educated, move to cities and empower women. Meanwhile, the moral responsibility is on us to demonstrate how our quality of life can be sustained within planetary boundaries.

#Agriculture.

The agro-industry sector is feeding people and starving the planet. In 1962, one farmer fed 25.8 persons; today it is 155. But our mechanistic, chemical-intensive methods are turning biologically rich soil into sterile dirt. As a result, nutrients in our foods have declined up to 80% since 1940. You have to eat 8 oranges today to get the same amount of vitamin A as our grandparents got from eating one. If we change the approach to regenerative, organic and biodynamic farming, agricultural land could absorb more than our annual carbon emissions each year. It's time to save our soil.

#Zoom.

The Oxford English Dictionary defines 'zoom' as an adverb meaning 'to move or go somewhere very fast'. Well, the videoconferencing company Zoom is surely living up to its name. Zoom, with a market capitalisation of $48.8 billion, is now worth more than the world's seven biggest airlines. The online communications platform was already fast becoming a new tech kid on the block, but COVID-19 gave it extra 'va va voom', with growth of 129% since 31 January, while the airlines have all shrunk between 48% and 73%. Post-crisis, it seems unlikely that we will zoom back to the skies.

#Wind.

Like our spirit, wind is invisible, yet we feel its effect. Sometimes, it blows a gentle breeze, light as a lover's kiss; other times, it whips up a raging gale, howling like a banshee. The secret of wind is that it is the seeker of balance, the bridge between differences. Air always moves from an area of high pressure to low pressure. Similarly, our spirit detects variance – such as between a mediocre present and an aspirational future – and it responds by creating movement, a motivation to act. We become inspired from the Latin meaning to 'breathe' or 'blow into'.

#Home.

Where do you feel most at home? We think of home as a place – and often it is – but when we reflect more deeply, we find that home is built around relationships. It's where you can connect with family and friends, or with nature. It's where you feel grounded and rooted, secure enough to branch out, to blossom and bear fruit. Home is your centre, where you can remove all the masks and simply be yourself. It is a wellspring where you can tap into your purpose and commune with your spirit. Home kindles the warm hearth of love.

#Things.

Every day, we buy things, use things and throw away things – often without knowing what they're made of, where they came from or what will happen after they're discarded. A pioneering tech company called EVRYTHNG wants to change that by giving every product a virtual profile, accessible from the cloud. By simply scanning the QR code from our phone, we will learn more about the product's life story. GoodGuide had a similar idea years ago and has rated 75,000 products on health and safety. Many don't care, but for those who do, it's another step towards supply chain transparency.

#Means.

Do the ends justify the means? Should we experiment on animals to test product safety? Should we experiment on humans to advance science, like the 'twins study' in the documentary 'Three Identical Strangers'? Should we destroy nature or abuse animals to feed a growing population and our insatiable appetite for more stuff? Some are false trade-offs. We can test products without animal cruelty and advance science without human guinea-pigs. We can feed people and make products without degrading nature or torturing animals. Yet governments, companies, scientists and consumers regularly use convenient ends to justify unacceptable means.

#Cars.

The auto industry is in free-fall – but more sustainable alternatives may be bucking the trend. Global car sales are expected to fall at least 20% in 2020 versus 2019. In April 2020, passenger car sales in Europe were down 78% year-on-year, and 66% from March to April 2020. Meanwhile Hertz, the 102-year old car rental company with 38,000 employees has filed for bankruptcy. In contrast, Tesla had its best first quarter performance ever, the e-scooter market is booming and online used car retailer Vroom just announced a stock market listing. Is the pandemic tipping us into more sustainable transport?

#Knowledge.

Ignorance may be bliss, but knowledge is a well of discovery that never runs dry. To care about nature or people, first we need to know about them. And the more we know, the more we are inspired. A single bacterium possesses about 10 million bits of genetic information; an insect one to 10 billion. By studying extremophile organisms, the health of soils, the acorn's encoded secrets, the pollination of lavender, the dance of honeybees, the flight of flamingos, the intelligence of pigs and the respiration of forests, we cultivate awe and respect. We learn to value life more.

#Regenerative.

Every year, the social and environmental costs of US agriculture is $85 billion. The decades-long drive for efficiency has optimised food output, instead of food quality, soil health, carbon absorption, animal welfare, biodiversity protection, and smallholder farmer livelihoods. Regenerative agriculture is the way to reverse these impacts, turning societal and environmental costs into benefits. But, as a recent report by Forum for the Future notes, scaling the solution faces multiple barriers, such as lack of market incentives, government support and customer demand. Given the size of the prize (and the cost of failure), we must persevere.

#Soap.

The humble bar of soap is enjoying something of a renaissance – and so it should. Even before COVID-19, the simple act of teaching children around the world to wash their hands can save a million deaths a year. There are also huge environmental benefits if we choose solid bars of soap, rather than liquids or gels. A comparative life cycle assessment found that we use six times more liquid soap per wash, and the bar has a carbon footprint ten times lower. Factor in the impact of plastic packaging waste and the soap bar becomes the clear sustainable choice.

#Fringes.

If you sometimes feel like you're on the fringe, fear not, for fringes are fabulous places. Roadside fringes are where poppies bloom and hedge fringes are where birds nest. It is on the fringes that change is catalysed. The mainstream is like a neatly tended grass lawn, where everything and everyone unorthodox are regarded as invasive weeds, to be strangled, mowed or poisoned. Yet even manicured gardens have their fringes, where biodiversity thrives. So too in society, where activists, entrepreneurs and changemakers breathe new life into dysfunctional ways and outdated ideas. So be on the fringe and be proud.

#Justice.

Anyone who claims to be an advocate for sustainable development should stand in solidarity with the #BlackLivesMatter movement. Injustice and the abuse of power are at the root of many of the sustainability crises we face. But when it's as blatant as George Floyd's murder by an American police officer and the persistent pattern of racist police brutality against Black people, we must insist on full accountability, justice and wholesale institutional reform. Sadly, this reminds me of the way white-supremacist police abused their power during apartheid in South Africa. Now is the time to demonstrate ethical leadership.

#Provisions.

Patagonia is getting into food. Isn't this the best sustainability news of 2020? Founder CEO Yvon Chouinard, a self-confessed 'doom-bat about humanity's prospects if we continue on the path we're on now', has concluded that selling more sustainable outdoor clothing and gear isn't good enough. Now, Patagonia Provisions will champion regenerative organic agriculture to grow and sell 'deeply flavourful, nutritious foods' that 'build soil health, ensure animal welfare and protect agricultural workers' – 'foods that are a key part of the solution instead of the problem', with a new triple bottom line: food, water, love. Are you a fan yet?

#Faith.

In times of doubt and destruction, of strain and struggle, it is important to have faith. But let us not see faith as blind believing. Faith is an active formula. It is believing in a better future, knowing that so many are working tirelessly to make it happen. It is believing in the goodness of people knowing that, despite the exceptions, billions are showing compassion and generosity every day all around the world. Faith means knowing the potential of people to grow, situations to change and nature to regenerate. And then using that knowledge to take positive action today.

#Competencies.

The biologist E.O. Wilson says that an ideal scientist must think like a poet, work like a clerk and write like a journalist. I believe that applies to anyone trying to make a positive impact on the world, as many sustainable development professionals are. We need to think creatively, to imagine better solutions to complex problems. Then we need to work systematically, to gather the evidence and build a compelling case for action. And finally, we need to be effective storytellers when we write or communicate in other ways about the benefits of changing the status quo.

#Environment.

The environment is everything that encircles us. This is the literal yet rather profound meaning that derived from early 17th century Old French *en* and *viron* (circle). When the word was introduced into the English language in 1827 by Thomas Carlisle, he elaborated the concept to mean 'the aggregate of the conditions in which a person or thing lives', similar to the German word 'umgebung'. These etymological roots remind us that the environment was always about nested living systems, including not only people and all other organisms but also their complex and dynamic relationships: the incredible web of life.

#Rain.

You wake up and it's raining. How does that make you feel? Do you grumble about the bad weather? Rain is a gift. All life depends on its nourishment. Rain irrigates our crops, fills our dams, washes our streets and rejuvenates our gardens. That should be reason enough to celebrate. But there is something more. Rain awakens our senses, as we breathe in its petrichor: that unique earthy scent of rain on dry soil, created as plant oils and soil bacteria react with water and release their perfumes. Rain replenishes our body, stimulates our mind and quenches our spirit.

#Panther.

Black Panther is more than just a superhero film. Based on a Stan Lee character who first appeared in the Fantastic Four comics in 1966, it has become the 12th highest grossing film of all time since its 2018 release, collecting $1.34 billion at the box office. It is a brilliant film with a fabulous soundtrack, but its significance is much greater. Not only is the superhero (and most of the cast) Black, the action is set in Wakanda, a mythical African country with technology vastly superior to the West, challenging prevailing attitudes about Africa. Change begins with imagination.

#Mariculture.

We need to change from being ocean hunters to being farmers. The agro-industrial approach to fishing has decimated the oceans. Some fish stocks, like Atlantic cod, already collapsed in the 1990s, while the global catch of wild seafood flatlined 20 years ago. One sustainable alternative is cultivating mussels in the ocean. Not only are they extremely healthy, packed with protein, fat and essential nutrients, they also grow fast with zero resource inputs – no feeds, no fertilisers, no fresh water. Mussels are the Buddhas of the deep, filtering and purifying 5,000 gallons a year as they breathe in and out.

#PPE.

What the world needs now is love, sweet love – but also PPE, and lots of it. That's tough to hear for sustainability advocates who've been in the trenches battling the pandemic of single-use plastic for the past few years. Just when we seemed to be turning the tide on throw-away packaging, a PPE tsunami is heading straight for shore. But the war is not yet lost. The world's first COVID-safe, recyclable, compostable, plastic-free visors – made from FSC paper board and transparent PEFC cellulose from wood pulp – have been launched by A Plastic Planet together with Reelbrands and Transcend Packaging Ltd.

#Ducklings.

I enjoyed reading John Elkington's book, Green Swans: The Coming Boom in Regenerative Capitalism. The metaphor is an elegant riff on Nassim Taleb's black swans, which are unpredictable, rare, high-impact events with severe consequences. Green swans are the opposite – positive exponential changes. Elkington plays with the concept, imagining black swans with green feathers and vice versa. I like his notion of ugly ducklings, referencing Hans Christian Anderson's fairy tale. This means that green swan entrepreneurs may not be immediately recognisable, until they grow out of their fledgling feathers. Welcome to the hobby of sustainability birdwatching.

#Cranberries.

How much do you know about cranberries? It turns out they may be one of the most sustainable crops in the world. I didn't know that, just like I had no idea that cranberries grow best in boggy, water-soaked soil. Every acre of cranberries needs 5.5 acres of surrounding marshland, so in effect, you have farmers preserving precious wetlands. Ocean Spray Cranberries, a $2 billion cooperative (I didn't know that either) recently became the first agricultural company to have all its 700 farms certified as 100% sustainable by the Sustainable Agriculture Initiative Platform (SAI Platform). This is farm-to-fork regenerative agriculture in action.

#Possibilist.

You don't have to be a blind optimist. Instead, you can choose to be a clear-eyed possibilist. Like the late great Hans Rosling, founder of Gapminder Foundation and author of Factfulnessness, a possibilist believes that a better future is possible – and that we need to work hard to make it happen. For example, a new University of California, Berkeley report finds that it's possible for the US to reach 70% renewable electricity by 2030 and 90% by 2035. Since 2010, the cost of utility-scale solar power has dropped 82% and onshore wind by 39%. What is possible in your future?

#Risk.

We live in a world where 'risk' has become a dirty word – something to be avoided at all costs. We encounter warnings against risk at every turn: at work, at home, on the roads, on products, in the media. But sometimes taking risks is the way to get the most out of life. As Ben Fogle tells it in his book 'Up: My Journey to the Top of Everest', without risk we cannot grow, we cannot improve, we cannot experience. In fact, we are in danger of never really living. Will you step out of your comfort zone today?

#Beaches.

Do you like beaches? I'm not one for frolicking in the surf and baking in the sun but give me a long walk along the beach any day. Beach walking is, to me, a kind of meditation. Gazing at the distant tranquil horizon. Contemplating the calming blue expanse of water, with its ruffles and frills of white. Listening to the rhythmic churning and crashing of the waves, as the ocean breathes in and out. Walking barefoot on the shore and feeling the sand between my toes and shell fragments massaging my soles. And with each step, recharging my soul.

#Ambition.

My simple test for separating sustainability pioneers from pretenders is to look at the extent of their admission (about the scale and urgency of our global challenges and their complicity in these) and ambition (about setting bold strategic goals that will transform not only themselves but society as well). One arena where both elements are in dire need is climate change. Here, the Climate Ambition Alliance gives us some hope, with 73 countries, 14 regions, 398 cities, 768 businesses and 16 investors committing to achieve net-zero CO_2 emissions by 2050. Combining ambition and societal consciousness leads to transformation.

#Unicorns.

Who will be the next Google, or Tesla, or Alibaba – and could they be a champion for sustainability? Spotting baby unicorns is rare – some might even say impossible. But CB Insights has an algorithm that has scored a few hits in the past. Its 2015 Future Unicorns list included Postmates Inc., Dollar Shave Club and HelloFresh, which all went on to become billion-dollar companies. Their new top 50 list is dominated by tech start-ups, which is not unexpected. I like the look of the digital health contenders like Doctor On Demand, Lyra Health and Capsule. Others too, somewhere over the rainbow.

#Jobs.

If you want to win an election, be sure to use the words job creation. And if you want to lose it, talk about climate change. At least, that's how it used to be. Now, research cited by McKinsey & Company shows that government spending on either energy efficiency or renewable energy is likely to create three times as many jobs as the same investment in fossil fuels. So why do governments still spend $5 trillion every year in fossil fuel subsidies worldwide? The most plausible explanation is corporate lobbying by coal, oil and gas companies – a form of state capture.

#Writedown.

Is the sun setting on the fossil fuels industry? BP will write down between $13 billion and $17.5 billion in the next quarter. The reason, says BP, is that the pandemic has weakened long-term demand for energy and will speed the transition to renewables. BP also revised assumptions about the 2030 carbon emissions price from $40 to $100 per ton. Could this be a first sign of fossil fuel stranded assets? Scientists estimate that a third of oil reserves, half of gas reserves and more than 80% of coal reserves must remain unburned to meet the Paris Climate Agreement.

#Hydroponics.

Did you know that the best basil in the world comes from Genoa, Italy – and the best tasting crop that chefs remember was from 1997? So that's the microclimate that Square Roots simulates in their shipping container hydroponic gardens. The company, co-founded by Kimbal Musk (Elon's brother), is part of the urban farming, real food and sustainable agriculture movements. Hydroponic systems grow leafy greens in vertical stacks, drip fed by liquid nutrients with little water, no soil, no weeds and no chemical pesticides or herbicides. If there is a pest infestation, they just simulate a Mohave desert climate. Ingenious.

#Fences.

Grameen Bank founder Muhammad Yunus told me some years ago that people don't need to be lifted out of poverty; if you remove the barriers, they will come out for themselves. It's the same with bringing nature back. In the 1950s, China constructed a railway – along with a fence – across the Gobi Desert. The Mongolian gazelles and khulan wild asses soon disappeared, their natural range cut off. Now, 65 years later, the Wildlife Conservation Society removed a short 2,300-foot section of fencing. And surprise, surprise, the gazelles and khulan are back. Take down more fences and wildlife will return.

#Storytelling.

We are all storytellers – and the better we are, the more impact we have in the world. Humans have evolved to communicate in symbols and look for patterns. Together, these make stories. Whether we are promoting a brand or campaigning on an issue, we are telling a story. There are three keys to effective storytelling. First, emotions beat intellect every time; we want to feel more than to think. Second, archetypes (prototypical characters, behaviours or forces) are powerful; we want our lives reflected. Third, coherence matters; we want a story to make sense. Ready? Once upon a time …

#Compass.

Unilever's new 10-year Compass strategy replaces the transformational Sustainable Living Plan that was the legacy of former CEO Paul Polman. There was some concern that his successor, Alan Jope, would give sustainability less priority. First indications are that those fears are unfounded. Along with establishing a €1bn Climate & Nature Fund, Unilever has committed to a deforestation-free supply chain by 2023, to have all its product formulations biodegradable by 2030 while implementing water stewardship programmes for local communities in 100 locations, and to have net zero emissions products by 2039. These are ambitious goals. Let's hope others follow their lead.

#Pollinators.

Birds, bees, wasps, hoverflies, bats – these are the world's pollinators, to which we can now add another species: humans. The total economic value of pollination globally is estimated to be €153 billion, nearly 10% of global agricultural production. But now, with 40% of insect species in decline and at risk of dying out around the world, in some parts of rural China like Hanyuan county, farmers are painstakingly pollinating by hand, using a stick with chicken feathers tied to the end. This is a tragic portent for what could become the new normal, unless we protect and restore the pollinators' habitats.

#Patents.

The world is desperate for a COVID-19 vaccine – and more than 20 biotech and pharmaceutical companies are working round-the-clock to deliver in 2021. These companies should be able recover all costs for the time, effort and resources they are pouring into developing safe and effective treatments for the virus, but should they be allowed to profit from the pandemic? More specifically, should they be allowed to patent their discoveries? When Jonas Salk developed the first successful polio vaccine in the 1950s, he was asked who owned the patent. His answer: 'There is no patent. Could you patent the sun?'

#Prometheus.

In Greek mythology, Prometheus is a Titan who steals fire from the gods and gives it to humanity. But what if we could 'steal' carbon from the atmosphere and turn it into fuels? That is the mission of Prometheus Fuels, who will launch their carbon neutral fuel on the market late in 2020. Investor BMW i Ventures calls this a 'game changer' – and they may be right. It will take at least a decade for people to replace their fossil fuel cars with electric vehicles, and if we want to avoid climate breakdown, we simply can't wait that long.

#Neutral.

Don't be fooled by the delaying tactics of companies. They can (and indeed they must) go climate neutral – and the most surprising thing is how affordable it is, for them and their customers. Unilever just committed to carbon labelling all of their products, following in the footsteps of Oatly and Quorn Foods, Inc. According to Climate Neutral, the certification company behind the label, an average running shoe that sells for $120 emits 20 kg CO_2e and would only cost $0.12 to offset; a $225 winter jacket would add $0.09 to the price; and a $60,000 electric SUV would cost $81 more.

#Clarity.

We live in an age of obfuscation – truth is turgid, morals are malleable, and compromise is commonplace. That's why clarity has become a rare and precious gift. I was reminded of this when listening to Greta Thunberg's poignant new podcast. The power of her message is not its novelty or nuance, but its simplicity and sincerity. Greta brings clarity: the climate emergency is crystal clear; so too the farcical failure of leadership. In her words, nature doesn't negotiate; the laws of physics don't compromise; science does not lie. Such clarity gives focus – and focus must lead to bold action.

#Music.

One of life's greatest and most beautiful mysteries is music. Where does it come from, and why does it move us so deeply? When a piece of music resonates, we are experiencing something deeply personal, something highly individual and reassuringly collective. We feel emotionally affected and affirmed, our senses sway in sync, our heart beats in time, our mind absorbs the lyrics, our spirit rises and falls on the waves of sound. Music, with or without words, is one of the most powerful forms of storytelling. And as Playing For Change reminds us, music can bring the world together.

#Offshore.

As the land becomes more crowded and degraded, we will increasingly turn to the sea – less as a living space and more as a zone of production. Today, we have offshore platforms primarily for deep sea oil and gas extraction and wind farms. In the near future, we will most likely move to multi-purpose offshore platforms that combine wind, solar and wave energy generation, aquaculture farming, hydrogen production, ship servicing and even maritime tourism. Sustainable designs will be key – such as those modelled by the EU funded MERMAID project – to avoid simply transferring existing terrestrial impacts to the oceans.

#Floating.

The disruption of supply chains during the COVID19 pandemic is bringing back the thousand-year-old farming practice of floating gardens in Mexico. These chinampas gardens were built by the Aztecs and are one of the most productive agricultural methods, with up to seven harvests per year. The farmers grow greens, herbs, flowers, fruits and milpa – corn, beans and squash – in the lake region of Xochimilco in the south of Mexico City. The land was largely abandoned after the devastating 1985 earthquake, but now it's making a comeback as a trusted, local source of organic, healthy food with a cultural heritage.

#ESG.

Sustainable and responsible investments that are screened on environmental, social and governance (ESG) criteria are less risky and outperform the market in both the short- and long-term, according to analysis of ESG funds in America and Europe by S&P Global Market Intelligence and Morningstar. And they are booming, reaching over $10 billion in Q1 of 2020 in the US. Now the Trump administration wants to shut them down with new regulations to prevent pension fund managers from investing in ESG products unless their decision is based on 'material economic considerations under generally accepted investment theories'. This is not okay.

#Trucks.

California is changing the world again – this time on greening truck fleets. According to the recently passed Advanced Clean Truck rule, more than half of the trucks sold in California have to be zero emission vehicles by 2035; and by 2045, all new trucks must meet this standard. In 2018 California already set the requirement that all new public transit buses sold must be zero-emission starting in 2029. And even earlier, in the 1990s, it was California's lower emission regulations that led to breakthrough innovations in passenger electric vehicles, first by Japanese manufacturers and followed by American and German automakers.

#SDGs.

The 2020 SDG Index is out, ranking countries on their Sustainable Development Goals progress. More interesting than the ranking (1 Sweden, 2 Denmark, 3 Finland) is the new pilot COVID Index (1 South Korea, 2 Latvia, 3 Australia) and analysis on which SDGs are worst affected by COVID-19 (SDGs 1, 2, 3, 8 and 10). Their Six Transformations are also a helpful framing: 1. Education, Gender, and Inequality, 2. Health, Wellbeing, and Demography, 3. Energy Decarbonization and Sustainable Industry, 4. Sustainable Food, Land, Water and Oceans, 5. Sustainable Cities and Communities, 6. Harnessing the Digital Revolution for Sustainable Development.

#LEDs.

The switch from incandescent to LED lightbulbs is already world-changing - and it's about to get even better. An average LED uses around 6 watts of electricity per hour and lasts 50,000 hours, compared with incandescent bulbs that use 50 watts and only last 1,200 hours. That's a 6-ton carbon saving per bulb. Now scientists have come up with a new biomimicry design inspired by the microscopic jagged surface of firefly abdomens, which look like a series of lopsided pyramids or factory roofs when magnified. Creating the same uneven surface on LEDs could increase the light they emit by 50%.

#Pockets.

We have reduced nature to pockets of green in the midst of patchwork farms, concrete cities and asphalt streets. But pockets can contain hidden treasures. Japanese botanist Akira Miyawaki has introduced the idea of pocket forests. Planting dense clusters of diverse native trees has a remarkable effect. These mini urban forests grow 10 times faster, have 100 times more biodiversity and store 40 times more carbon than conventional forests. The small, local scale of pocket forests means that they can be grown in schools, parks, campuses, corporate offices; or even on roofs, at factories or in suburban gardens.

#Thirsty.

When we think of Carl Sagan's Pale Blue Dot and Sir David Attenborough's Blue Planet, we are conjuring up images of our beautiful watery home. But the impression that water is abundant on Earth is misleading. If all the world's water were gathered into a sphere, it would be 11% the size of the Earth; fresh water would be 2% – and since 1900, freshwater withdrawals have increased six-fold. Already, the WRI estimates a quarter of the world's population face extremely high levels of water stress, and MIT research predicts this may rise to 50% by 2050. Let's get water-wise.

#Buckets.

Every day a woman fetches water from a river in two buckets, each suspended on the end of a wooden pole across her shoulders. One day, she overhears the buckets talking. 'I'm old and leaky' says the one. 'I fear I will be replaced.' So the woman asks the rickety bucket: 'What do you see on our daily journey?' 'When I'm empty on the way there,' the bucket replies, 'I see only barren ground.' 'And on the way back when you're full?' she asks. 'Then I see beautiful wildflowers.' She nods and smiles: 'Your leaking made that beauty possible.'

#Landscapes.

Have you ever thought of your life or your career as a landscape? It's an instructive thought experiment. What does the landscape look like? Does it meander like a river? If so, what do the twists and turns represent? What have been turbulent rapids and calm stretches, abrupt waterfalls and dam barriers along the way? When did you journey over steep mountains and through shadowed valleys? Where did you find places of community in which to settle or areas of wilderness in which to wander? Each landmark is important – and together they make the unique terrain of your life.

#Concrete.

The 'concrete jungle' is usually a disparaging reference to cities where nature has been obliterated by buildings and asphalt. But what if we could build with concrete that is living, rather than inert? That's what scientists at University of Colorado Boulder have been working on. By mixing cyanobacteria with sand and gelatine, they have produced a material with the potential to self-heal, absorb pollution and even glow in the dark. The bio-concrete's lower carbon footprint could help to tackle the cement industry's climate impacts, which currently account for 8% of global CO_2 emissions. These are the beginnings of regenerative construction.

#Reset.

Those who are expecting society or the economy to transform post COVID will be disappointed – but they will not be wrong. The calls for a Great Reset or for Green Bailouts will find traction in some places, but not in others. Most will try to get back to normal; to restore business-as-usual. But do not mistake the lack of visible changes for a lack of change. The system has already changed irrevocably – and some of the most profound and impactful transformations will be from small shifts (in mindset or actions) that even now are rippling and accumulating across the system.

#Haircuts.

What was your first post-lockdown haircut like? Mine was five months in the making, and I have once again reverted from long-haired hippie to ship-shape professional. It's surprising how this small act of personal grooming restores a sense of order, a feeling of returning to normality. I confess I'm an impatient hairdressing client. The sooner I can get in and out, the better – preferably with no blow-drying, no gels, no wax. But this time, I was reminded that having our hair cut is an act of simple kindness and conscious attention. Caring about others starts with caring about ourselves.

#Imperfection.

When John Legend sings about 'all your perfect imperfections' in his song 'All of Me', he is unknowingly drawing on the Japanese philosophical practice of wabi-sabi. Richard Powell, a wabi-sabi scholar, says this perspective on life acknowledges three simple realities: nothing lasts, nothing is finished, and nothing is perfect. The spirit of wabi-sabi is made visible in the beautiful Japanese art of kintsugi, where the cracks in old pottery are filled with gold-dusted lacquer to highlight, rather than hide, its imperfections. As the incomparable Leonard Cohen noted: there is a crack in everything; that's how the light gets in.

#Cotton.

Soon, we may avoid using toxic, chemical dyes for textiles, thanks to a scientific breakthrough that allows cotton to grow naturally in different colours. According to Trusted Clothes, 10-15% of dyes are released into the environment during the dyeing process, causing 40,000 to 50,000 tons of annual chemical pollution by the global textile industry. Now the Australian science organisation CSIRO has discovered that adding certain genes can produce yellow, orange and purple cotton. Surely this is an example of using genetic modification for a better, more sustainable solution. Isn't it time that our views on GMOs became more nuanced?

#Reporting.

The reason financial reporting works is because it's standardised. Non-financial reporting (also called CSR, sustainability, ESG or SDG reporting) isn't there yet, but not for lack of trying. The trail includes the Toxic Release Inventory (1986), EMAS (1993), GRI (1999), AA1000 (1999), CDP (2000), A4S (2004), IIRC (2010), SASB (2011), r3.0 (2012), Future Fit Benchmark (2016) and Value Balancing Alliance (2019). Now, GRI and SASB are collaborating to achieve coherent messaging, and the World Economic Forum has a project with the Big 4 accounting firms called 'Toward Common Metrics and Consistent Reporting of Sustainable Value Creation'. It's all progress.

#Rosetta.

When the Rosetta Stone was discovered in 1799 with identical text in hieroglyphic, Demotic and Ancient Greek, it became the key to deciphering the hieroglyphics. I feel like we need multiple Rosetta Stones for sustainability today – translations (and translators) that will make sustainable development understandable. What does it mean for young people, old people, those in developing countries, or rich countries, for business leaders, policymakers and activists? Simply repeating the message in our own language – be that scientific, political, commercial or activist – is unlikely to achieve the unity we need to take urgent, ambitious action at a global scale.

#Loop.

After a COVID-induced delay, the zero waste shopping platform Loop has launched in the UK (it already runs in France and the US). TerraCycle works with manufacturers like Heinz, Coca Cola, Unilever, Danone and Nivea, retailers like Tesco and logistics companies like DHL and DPD, to enable shoppers to purchase food, drink, health, beauty and cleaning products online and then to return the packaging – either from home using an online request for pick-up, or at one of the 2,500 DPD collection points. Tesco hopes this will help remove one billion pieces of plastic packaging from its UK stores by 2021.

#Ecovalue.

How do you create 400 million jobs in the wake of a pandemic, while generating $10tn in annual business value by 2030? According to the World Economic Forum's new 'Future of Nature and Business' report, it's by making $2.7tn in green investments, giving a 370% return. The downside of not doing so is equally compelling: the destruction of nature is threatening over half of global GDP. The opportunities range from retrofitting cities for ecoefficiency ($825bn benefit) to better management of wild fish ($172bn). Instead, we see $151bn in bailouts for the fossil fuel industry. Not investing in sustainability today is economic madness.

#Giants.

Those who declare themselves giants, seldom are. As we enter the circus season of the US general election, it is worth remembering that 'bigging' yourself up does not make you a giant. Rather let us recall the words of Sir Isaac Newton, an undisputed intellectual giant, who famously wrote in 1676, 'If I have seen further, it is by standing on the shoulders of giants.' This was the spirit of another giant, Nelson Mandela, a servant of the people who likened leadership to being a shepherd, allowing the nimble to go ahead, letting others follow and guiding from behind.

#Synergetics.

Studying the shapes and patterns of nature is inherently fulfilling, but also deeply insightful. The polymath Buckminster Fuller, best known for his geodesic dome design, called this 'synergetics'. Fuller, who was expelled from Harvard twice, looked for recurring mathematical relationships in nature and applied them to fields as diverse as geometry, thermodynamics, chemistry, psychology, architecture, economics, philosophy and theology. The broad sweep of synergetics prefigured much of what is today the science of living systems, especially the phenomenon of emergence, where the behaviour of the total system cannot be predicted by the behaviour of its individual parts.

#Shactivism.

Shareholder activism has long been a strategy of the responsible and sustainable investment movement. But when BlackRock adopts this approach, as the world's biggest investor ($7.43 trillion assets under management), you know that the game has changed. In their recent investment stewardship report, they disclose how they have voted to replace directors or support shareholder ESG proposals for 53 companies (with a combined market cap of $669 billion) and placed another 191 on notice for action in 2021 if they do not make substantial progress. Blackrock's environmental 'shactivism' (including on climate change) went up 289% in the past year.

#Inclusivity.

Inclusion of diverse groups in society and organisations doesn't just happen spontaneously. Quite the opposite. Tribal dynamics mean that people often seek out others like themselves and exclude anyone different. The Global Inclusivity Report 2020 highlights societal barriers, notably race discrimination and poverty, and workplace challenges, where biases in recruitment or promotions, leadership attitudes and gender discrimination play a key role. The benefits are compelling: promoting different ways of thinking, a culture of openness and learning, creativity, productivity, motivation and the creation of economic value. To achieve these, we must make diversity an action not an adjective.

#Bags.

The battle of the bags rages on – more specifically, on what constitutes a sustainable shopping bag. But surely the answer is simple? Just bring your own reusable bag. There are two problems with that. First, most shoppers don't. And second, life cycle assessments show that bags need to be reused between 37 times (for plastic) and 1,000 times (for cotton) to have a lower ecological footprint than single-use plastic bags. That's why Walmart, Target, and CVS Health are working with Closed Loop Partners on the Beyond the Bag Initiative, which is a call for innovators to reinvent single use shopping bags.

#Bountiful.

Nature is rich in bounty, full of precious treasure, generous rewards and – in accordance with the Latin root of the word – pure goodness. Yet most of nature's gifts go undetected, ignored or get squandered. The winged bean of New Guinea contains more protein than cassava and potato, the wax gourd of tropical Asia grows an inch every three hours and reaches maturity in four days, the babassu palm from the Amazon (known locally as the 'vegetable cow') can produce 125 barrels of oil from 500 trees, and the serendipity berry from West Africa is 3,000 times sweeter than sucrose.

#Shade.

When you think about social justice, I bet you're not thinking about shade. In a recent TED Talk, Los Angeles mayor Eric Garcetti, who is chair of the C40 group of cities tackling climate change, said something totally unexpected: 'shade is an equity issue'. Around the world, the poorest, most marginalised communities live in areas with no trees and high levels of environmental degradation and pollution. Environment almost always touches on social inequalities. The lack of shade is a proxy for numerous other overlooked ecological injustices. Greening cities must mean bringing nature and a clean environment to the underserved.

#Lichen.

Did you know that lichen – which covers around 6% of the Earth's surface – is a symbiotic composite organism. It emerges from algae or cyanobacteria living among the filaments of fungi. Both organisms benefit – protection, moisture and nutrients in exchange for carbohydrates produced by photosynthesis. The co-operating organisms can live separately, but in a different form. When they collaborate as lichen, they are neither plant nor fungus. Lichen is remarkable in other ways too: it can survive the vacuum of space and long periods of drought. It's also one of nature's most beautiful colour palettes. You've got to love lichen.

#Microphilia.

Sometimes focusing on the big picture makes us blind to the myriad tiny worlds each contains: the macro obscures the micro. A Monet painting of his home garden at Giverny is a wonder to behold. But step in closer and the daubs of paint take on a life of their own. A single flower or water lily is a microcosmos of swirling colours; the bark on a tree reveals a rugged terrain of textures. The same is true in nature, whether in your own garden, a favourite park, or pristine wilderness area, endless revelations of miniature delights await you.

#Leather.

The switch to sustainable fashion materials is well underway – and plant-based leather is the next big thing. Making alternatives to animal skin has brought eco entrepreneurs out of the woodwork, with faux leather materials being produced from mushrooms (Amadou and Mycoworks), pineapple leaves (Piñatex), cork (Corkor) – and the newest kids on the block: eggplant skins (chef Omar Sartawi), cacti (Adriano Di Marti) and apple peels (Beyond Leather Materials ApS). They will all have to demonstrate that they can be as versatile and durable as hide-based leather. But for the animals, the environment and the climate, it's a challenge worth taking up.

#Awoken.

New research by UNGC and Russel Reynolds Associates finds three types of sustainability leader: the born believers (45%, with a passion for the environment or social issues fostered from an early age), the convinced (43%, where understanding of the strategic importance of sustainability grew as they advanced in their careers), and the awoken (12%, who had a pivotal moment of realisation, prompted by some major event or experience, that there was more to business than profit). We spend a lot of our time celebrating the believers and nurturing the convinced. But I expect a fresh crop of newly awoken post pandemic.

#Vaccine.

Of the 160 Coronavirus vaccines under development, five have successfully advanced to stage three trials among thousands of human volunteers. If all goes well, we will see government approvals before the end of 2020. Then an unprecedented supply chain effort will kick into high-gear to produce and distribute the vaccines. WEF estimates that between 10 and 19 billion vaccines will be needed globally. To put this in perspective, one billion children have been vaccinated in the world over the past 10 years. This will be a coming of age moment for blockchain technology, to ensure traceability and prevent fraud.

#Consequences.

Everything we do has consequences – but very few impacts are all bad, even if they seem that way at first. COVID-19 is having devastating impacts, but in time we may look back and see that it has changed key behaviours around air travel, appreciating nature, working remotely, switching to renewables and work-life balance. In my first book, Beyond Reasonable Greed, I used elephants as a metaphor for sustainable business. Elephants are matriarchal, intelligent and community-oriented, but can be destructive. Yet even these impacts create new pathways, access to food and niche habitats for others in the web of life.

#Aquaponics.

No doubt you're familiar with aquaculture and probably hydroponics too – but have you heard about aquaponics? Upward Farms recently raised $15 million for scaling its symbiotic agricultural model, in which the nitrogen-rich wastewater from fish tanks is used to fertilise leafy greens. This is a way to mimic what nature does, turning waste from one process into food for another. The jury is still out on whether this can be scaled in a sustainable way. Any intensive agriculture creates unintended and often unwanted impacts. But there are definitely community and environmental benefits from local, circular economy inspired food production.

#Caterpillars.

Most of us are caterpillars – and that's okay, because it means we are on the journey to becoming butterflies. Unfortunately, we live in a society that glorifies colourful, sleek, flighty butterflies – the celebrities, tycoons or politicians – without reminding us that they all started out as ordinary, pudgy, crawling caterpillars. We should be looking in the mirror and not seeing 'ugly', 'uninteresting' or 'slow achiever', but rather 'beautiful', 'fascinating' and 'in transformation'. Let's celebrate the caterpillars of this world – the tireless workers and hidden heroes, the resilient communities and invisible caregivers. Let's look at caterpillars and see their inner butterflies.

#Pando.

For the past 80,000 years, the Trembling Giant has lived at Fishlake National Forest, Utah, USA. This is no fantasy giant – it is the living, breathing kind. Its name, Pando, from the Latin meaning 'I spread', gives us a vital clue. Pando is a superorganism comprised of 45,000 quaking aspen trees, all genetically identical and sharing the same root system, spanning 107 acres and weighing 6,615 tons. Individual trees come and go, but the gentle giant lives on – except that today, Pando's life is under threat due to overgrazing by deer and elk. Let's protect and respect our elders.

www.ingramcontent.com/pod-product-compliance
Lightning Source LLC
Chambersburg PA
CBHW061949070426
42450CB00007BA/1105